AMERICA

AMERICA

PHOTOGRAPHS BY JAKE RAJS

FOREWORD BY JAMES A. MICHENER

RIZZOLI
NEW YORK

Pages 2–3: Farmland, Idaho

Page 4: Byers Lake and Mt. McKinley, Denali National Park, Alaska

Pages 6–7: San Francisco, California

Pages 10–11: Magnolia Gardens, South Carolina

Page 12: Space Shuttle *Discovery*, John F. Kennedy Space Center, Cape Canaveral, Florida

Pages 14–15: Acoma Pueblo, New Mexico

First published in the United States of America in 1990 by
RIZZOLI INTERNATIONAL PUBLICATIONS, INC.
300 Park Avenue South, New York, New York 10010

Photography copyright © 1990 Jake Rajs
Foreword copyright © 1990 James A. Michener

Library of Congress Cataloging-in-Publication Data
Rajs, Jake.
   America / photographs by Jake Rajs : foreword by James
A. Michener.
     p.   cm.
   ISBN 0-8478-1244-8
     1. United States—Description and travel—1981—Views.
I. Title.
E169.04.R34   1990
973.9'022'2—dc20   90-8169
                                                         CIP

Design by Gilda Hannah
Composition by Rainsford Type
Printed in Japan

To my father
whose vision of freedom
brought me to America

CONTENTS

OUR AMERICA   17
James A. Michener

WILDERNESS   22

FARMS AND TOWNS   90

SHORELINES   134

ROADWAYS   164

CITIES   188

OUR AMERICA

This book is a joyous celebration! Its nearly two hundred sparkling photographs remind us of the extraordinary land our nation occupies, and a review of them shows us how fortunate we are to live where we do.

Our nation is a mansion erected on three powerful pillars: the creative mix of our citizenry; the moral, political and economic principles which it built; and, basic to all else, the glorious land we have been able to occupy.

A principal fact about that land is its continental dimension, stretching as it does clear across North America, from the Atlantic to the Pacific. Most nations do not have the freedom of movement which comes from such magnitude. From birth we Americans are accustomed to hugeness of scale. We are not pinned down in a corner. We are free to range across an entire continent, taking our children where we will. And those children are free to construct their lives anywhere from Maine to California, from Oregon to Florida.

This bigness provides us with a spacious landscape in which to experiment, at times achieving wonders that would not be possible in a cramped area, at other times making colossal mistakes, as in our farming programs, yet always able to survive and bounce back, partly because we are so large that we can absorb bad knocks.

Our land is not only spacious, it is also unbelievably rich: coal in the east, iron ore in the north, gold in the west, oil in the southwest, trees everywhere, fields so vast and fertile they could feed most of the world, and copious supplies of water to nourish them.

I have sometimes thought that the significant difference between Australia and the United States can be explained only by the differing gifts of nature.

The two countries are of comparable size, Australia at just under three million square miles, the United States somewhat above three and a half. But Australia, on her relatively deprived land can support only fifteen million people, while the United States can provide for more than two hundred and forty million. A principal reason for this vast difference is that down the middle of our nation flows the sovereign Mississippi River with its major tributaries: the far-reaching Missouri, the powerful Ohio, the quiet Tennessee, the wandering Arkansas, plus their networks: the Yellowstone, the Platte, Allegheny, Kentucky, Red. Rip that intricate river system from the heartland of our nation, and the states lying inland from the Atlantic and Pacific Oceans would be the Great American Desert. Like Australia, we would be able to support only a small population clinging to our two seacoasts, and numbering not in the hundreds of millions but in the tens. And with such limited numbers, the empty areas would not be able to supply markets for the industries of our coastal cities and manufacturing districts. We should be grateful that we are a big land, with adequate water, at least for the present.

Therefore I am glad to see among these handsome pictures a reminder of our almost limitless grain fields (117, South Dakota), our magnificent woodlands (66, California), our soaring mountains (82, Oregon) and our life-giving rivers (132, Minnesota). They remind us of our good fortune.

There are other corners of the earth comparably blessed by nature on which great civilizations have not arisen, and I believe the difference lies in the kinds of people who occupied our land.

America had the good fortune to be settled by people—those already here at the beginning and those who arrived later—who were sturdy, strong-minded, courageous and determined to preserve the riches and the freedom they found here.

It required tremendous heroism for our original Indians to leave their natal Siberia some forty thousand years ago, cross the Bering Ice Bridge then exposed, and wander down onto what would later become western America. There they multiplied, making the land and its natural features—rivers, lakes and buffalo—their own.

The first Europeans who arrived to share the land with them were a determined people: the rebellious English who placed their stamp upon the new nation, the daring French who in the earliest years explored where the English seemed afraid to venture, the sturdy, well-educated Germans and then, starting in the 1820s, that constant inflow of Europeans who rushed here to escape economic, social and military tyranny, that flood of patriots from Austria, Scandinavia, Russia, Poland, Italy and the Slavic states. We gathered jewels from the far corners of the earth.

Then came the industrious settlers from Asia: the Chinese, the Japanese, the Filipinos with their manifold skills. In my own lifetime, I have been involved intimately with new floods of settlers who have come here to seek our time-honored freedoms: the excellent Hungarians in 1956, the powerfully oriented Cubans in the 1960s, the Vietnamese of the 1970s. What a powerful mix of people!

Of major significance in our national life, always present, always contributing, were the Africans who arrived in slavery and fought their way to equality. They form a constant thread in our history, a noble one that gives our nation a distinctive quality.

Had this flood of settlers arrived in America barren of ideas, I doubt they could have accomplished much, even though they inherited a paradise. Fortunately, they reached our shores exploding with ideas, with moral convictions, with inventive concepts and with the courage to fight for what they believed. It was from this cauldron of seething convictions that our nation emerged.

The earliest settlers knew precisely what they wanted: freedom of religion, freedom to trade in new patterns, freedom to educate their children, freedom to move about and freedom from royal absolutism. Thus motivated, they erected here societies which enabled them to achieve the goals denied them at home. We were fortunate to have started our nation with such morally rigorous people, for their solid ideas would give direction to all that followed.

The people who started our nation believed in God, the prudence of Bible teaching, and the right of each man to worship as he saw fit. The convictions became so engrained in our national conscience that, when our founding fathers launched their Revolution in 1776, they sought divine guidance in their struggle against oppression. We are a nation brought into being by men and women of faith, and the simple New Hampshire church shown on page 124 bespeaks their rugged beliefs. The more ornate steeples which dominate the Maine village on page 158 represent church buildings across the land.

But the men who framed our Constitution had witnessed so much religious dictatorship and even persecution in their study of history, in both Europe and their own colonies, that they repeatedly refused in their Convention in Philadelphia in 1787 to allow any church-state relationship. Despite Benjamin Franklin's almost tearful plea that the delegates declare their work to have been done under divine guidance, they would not do so. In fact, they even refused to discuss the matter. Organized religion is not mentioned in the original Constitution, and the first provision of the later Bill of Rights is a caution against allowing the new Republic to establish a state religion, or to abridge such freedom of religion as already existed in the colonies. The men who established our nation wanted us to be a moral nation but not doctrinaire, and we have been determined to remain so.

From the beginning the character of our country has expressed itself in its social traditions: a wide variety of free churches, free-speaking newspapers, free public education, public roads and waterways, transportation probing into the remotest corners of the land, colleges, libraries, hospitals, museums, theaters, orchestras, local and national parks, plus a profusion of clubs like Boy and Girl Scouts for children, Rotary and Daughters of the American Revolution for grown-ups, Parent-Teacher Associations, support groups for local hospitals, the American Legion, labor unions, alumni who collect funds to support their universities, those worthy groups who protect defenseless children and animals and the excited citizens who support the political candidates of their choice or initiate and try to pass referendums.

No stranger could hope to understand the United States, unless she or he followed the contributions of these constructive groups. They are voluntary. Their members work without pay, and they are inspired by the highest principles of our national heritage. When I travel abroad, and see some heinous social injustice, I am apt to cry: "That would never be allowed in the United States!" by which I probably mean: "The good women of our town would not permit a condition like that to continue." And then I add: "Their busy husbands might ignore it, but their wives would press the issue." I am enormously proud of what the women of America have pressured their husbands to do.

A salvation of our country has been its ability to conduct a vigorous and at times almost violent political life—go to the polls on Tuesday, cast our vote, and on Wednesday morning say calmly: "All right! This time the other side won. Let them rule for four years, and then we'll take another crack at them." This commendable willingness to join forces the morning after a heated election is in stark contrast to the political behavior of many European and Asian nations in which the voting takes place on Sunday, but the real election begins next day when no clear-cut mandate has been delivered, and the various minority parties launch a three-week hassle to determine what coalition of disparate parties will govern, tenuously.

And our system of conferring immediate responsibility on the winning team is infinitely superior to the Latin American one of installing a civilian president, but then encouraging the military to throw him out and establish their own petty dictatorship. Orderly politics is the mark of a mature nation, and we are twice fortunate that our predecessors got us started right, and that we have preserved their admirable system.

In recent decades the economic life of any nation has assumed such dominating importance that many Americans have come to believe that the most valuable asset in our life is our system of semi-regulated capitalism. It seems to provide maximum welfare for the maximum number of people, and it has been the success of this system, in the United States and in the other democracies, that has revealed Communism to be such a deficient alternative. The older I grow the more respect I have for our American system, but I have certainly seen times when even it faltered. As a young man in the Great Depression, I witnessed so many things which needed correction that I might have become an extreme socialist, but I refrained because I believed that we had, as a people, the brains to make corrections. We did, and I lived to see many of the injustices which had worried me removed.

I have remained sensitive to social and economic injustice and today see many spots on our national fabric that cry out for cleaning up: a more stable money system, a reduced debt, a return to a goods-producing economy rather than a consuming one, greater productivity in our work force, wiser management at the top, the elimination of laws which allow and encourage any financial wizard to use junk securities to gain control of major producing companies, gut them for quick personal profit, then throw thousands of working men and women out of the jobs they had expected to last their lifetimes.

Two problems seem to supersede all others: the insidious terror of drugs and the growing gap between rich and poor, illustrated by the fact that even young people of good character and work habits cannot afford to own homes for their families, while many at the bottom of the social order can find no homes at all and must live on the streets. We should dedicate ourselves to the eradication of such impediments.

These exquisite photographs remind us of how precious our heritage is. The grandeur of our landscape is revealed in shots like those of the Grand Canyon (88, Arizona), Mt. McKinley (4, Alaska) and Sankaty Light (145, Massachusetts).

The appropriateness of how our ancestors built on their land is shown in the architectural simplicity of the rural church (92, Connecticut) and the stately grace of the plantation (122, Louisiana). While their plans for expansion and development are recognized in our great cities of today: Chicago, San Francisco, Detroit, Houston and New York (226, 190, 199, 188, 252).

The people who wander through these pages add color to their land: the lonely pool shooter (109, Arkansas), the taro farmer (118, Hawaii) and, best of all, the Navajo father forming an ideal cradle for his son (108, Arizona). I was fascinated by the shot of the Indianapolis speedway (217), because I could not figure out in which direction the two cars headed. Then it became clear. The top car has gone into a tire-burning spin, has made a hundred-and-eighty degree whirl, and is headed for disaster.

Because I cherish the animals who share America with me, I was delighted to see portraits of creatures about which I have written: the bald eagle of Alaska (67), the buffalo of South Dakota (84), the high-stepping heron (58, Texas), who could be the one who used to live in our backyard swamp; and the cloud of geese rising from the Maryland wildlife refuge a few miles from our home (52).

Repeated study of these photographs ought to instill in each of us a determination to leave our land in at least as good condition as when we received it . . . or better.

James A. Michener
Texas Center for Writers
Austin, Texas

In Wildness is the preservation of the world.
                              —Henry David Thoreau

WILDERNESS

Pages 22–23: Yellowstone National Park, Wyoming

Page 25: Reid Glacier, Glacier Bay National Park, Alaska

Pages 26–27: Mt. Rainier and Reflection Lake, Mt. Rainier National Park, Washington

Page 28: Badlands National Park, South Dakota

Page 29: Spider Rock, Canyon de Chelly National Monument, Navajo Nation, Arizona

Page 30: Badlands National Park, South Dakota

Page 31: Na Pali Coast, Kauai, Hawaii

Page 33: Waterfall, Hawaii, Hawaii

Page 34: Buffalo, Theodore Roosevelt National Park, North Dakota

Page 35: Wild horses, Theodore Roosevelt National Park, North Dakota

Pages 36–37: Crater Lake National Park, Oregon

Page 38: White Sands National Monument, New Mexico

Page 39: Potomac River, Arlington, Virginia

Page 41: Lake Powell, Gunsight Canyon, Glen Canyon
National Recreation Area, Utah/Arizona

Pages 42–43: Fall reflection, New Hampshire

Page 44 (above): Red Rock Canyon, Las Vegas area, Nevada

Page 44 (below): Bryce Canyon National Park, Utah

Page 45: Zion National Park, Utah

Pages 46–47: Great Smoky Mountains National Park,
Tennessee

Page 49: White House Ruin, Canyon de Chelly National Monument, Arizona

Pages 50–51: Canyon de Chelly National Monument, Navajo Nation, Arizona

Pages 52–53: Geese, Blackwater National Wildlife Refuge, Maryland

Page 55: Moose, Wonder Lake, Denali National Park, Alaska

Pages 56–57: Blue heron, Okefenokee National Wildlife Refuge, Georgia

Page 58: Blue heron, Caddo Lake, Texas

Page 59: White-tailed deer, Cades Cove, Great Smoky Mountains National Park, Tennessee

Pages 60–61: Red alders, Redwood National Park, California

Pages 62–63: Wildflowers, Brenham, Texas

Page 65: Autumn foliage, Adirondack Park, New York

Page 66: Jedediah Smith Redwoods State Park, California

Page 67 (above): Bald eagle, Haines, Alaska

Page 67 (below): Hoh Rain Forest, Olympic National Park, Washington

Pages 68–69: Carlsbad Caverns National Park, New Mexico

Pages 70–71: The Windows, Arches National Park, Utah

Page 73 (above): Elephant seals, Año Nuevo State Reserve, California

Page 73 (below): Alligator, Okefenokee National Wildlife Refuge, Georgia

Pages 74–75: Chilkoot Lake, Haines, Alaska

Page 76 (above): Yosemite National Park, California

Page 76 (below): Half Dome, Yosemite National Park, California

Page 77 (above): Matanuska Glacier, Alaska

Page 77 (below): Avalanche Lake, Adirondack Park, New York

Pages 78–79: The Dells, Prescott, Arizona

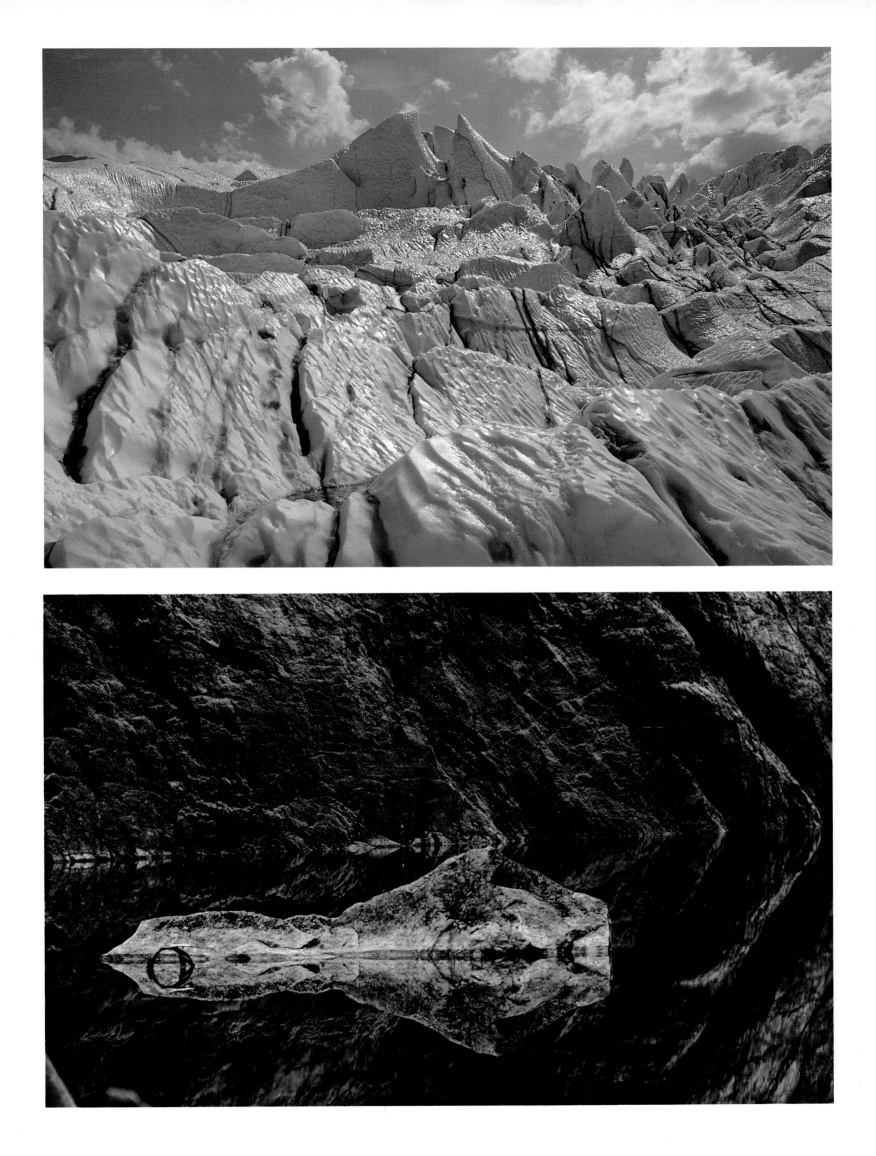

Page 81 (above): Snow geese, Bombay Hook National Wildlife Refuge, Delaware

Page 81 (below): Tundra swans, Lake Mattamuskeet, North Carolina

Page 82 (above): Mt. Hood and Lost Lake, Oregon

Page 82 (below): Lake Sherburne, Glacier National Park, Montana

Page 83 (above): Mt. Whitney, California

Page 83 (below): Snake River, Grand Teton National Park, Wyoming

Pages 84–85: Buffalo, Badlands National Park, South Dakota

Page 87: Sand and butte, Monument Valley, Navajo Nation, Arizona/Utah

Pages 88–89: Grand Canyon, Arizona

The farmers . . . are the founders of human civilization.
　　　　　　　　　　　　　　　　　—Daniel Webster

FARMS AND
TOWNS

Pages 90–91: Farm, Vermont

Pages 92–93: Church, Warren, Connecticut

Page 95: Amish woman at Sunday Prayer, Intercourse, Pennsylvania

Page 96 (above): Fredonia, Texas

Page 96 (below): Vicksburg, Mississippi

Page 97 (above): Opelika, Alabama

Page 97 (below): Yellowstone National Park, Wyoming

Pages 98–99: Saint Jerome Chapel, Taos Pueblo, New Mexico

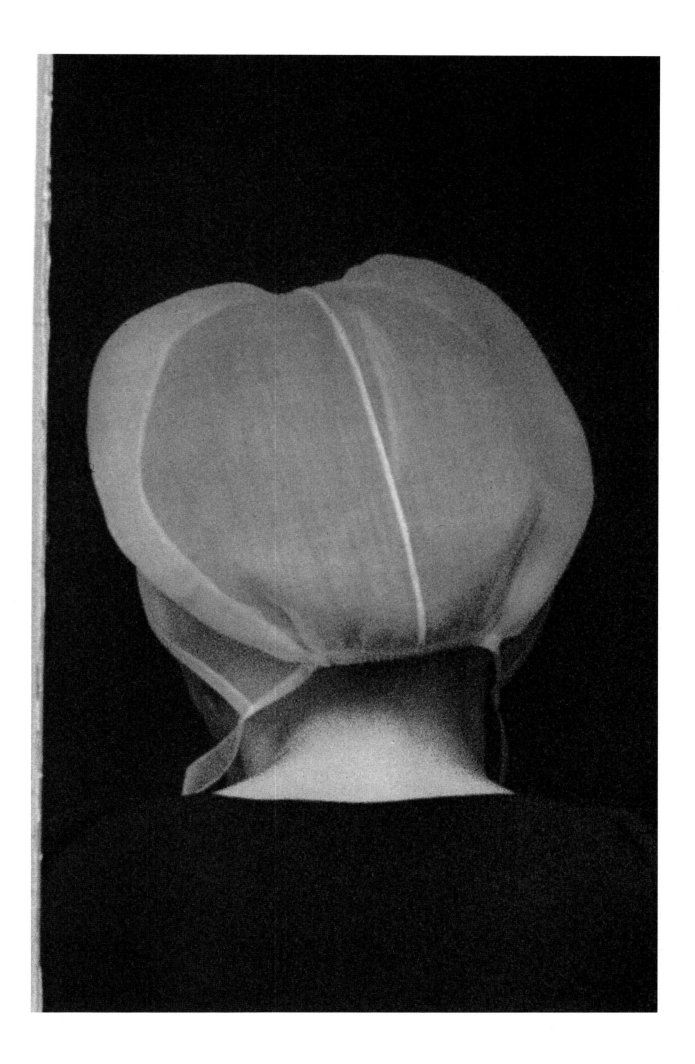

Page 100: National Fresh Water Fishing Hall of Fame, Hayward, Wisconsin

Page 101: Mountain View, Arkansas

Page 103 (above): Cranberry harvest, Wareham, Massachusetts

Page 103 (below): Cotton harvest, New Madrid, Missouri

Pages 104–105: Fall colors, New York

Pages 106–107: Flower farm, near Gilroy, California

Page 108: Father and child, Kayenta, Navajo Nation, Arizona

Page 109: Busters Recreation Hall, Mountain View, Arkansas

Pages 110–111: Farm, near Dover, Delaware

Page 113 (above): Barn and wildflowers, Alaska

Page 113 (below): Barn, Lake Champlain, Vermont

Pages 114–115: Sunflowers, South Charleston, Ohio

Page 116 (above): Tobacco farm, Lexington, Kentucky

Page 116 (below): Milo field, Missouri

Page 117 (above): Wheatfield, near Pomeroy, Washington

Page 117 (below): Silos, Scenic, South Dakota

Pages 118–119: Taro farmer, Keanae Peninsula, Maui, Hawaii

Page 121 (above): New Castle, Delaware

Page 121 (below): Eldorado, Iowa

Pages 122–123: Oak Alley Plantation, Vacherie, Louisiana

Pages 124–125: Church, Stark, New Hampshire

Page 126 (above): Chicken farm, Seaford, Delaware

Page 126 (below): Farmer, Kansas

Page 127 (above): Amish farm, near Dover, Delaware

Page 127 (below): Turkey farm, Fort Seybert, West Virginia

Pages 128–129: Chimney Rock, Nebraska

Page 130 (above): Farm, near Glen Haven, Michigan

Page 130 (below): Old gas station, Eufaula, Oklahoma

Page 131: South Royalton, Vermont

Pages 132–133: Headwaters of the Mississippi River, Bemidji, Minnesota

The river is within us, the sea is all about us;

The sea is the land's edge also, the granite

Into which it reaches, the beaches where it tosses

Its hints of earlier and other creation.

—T. S. Eliot

SHORELINES

Pages 134–135: La Push, Olympic National Park, Washington

Pages 136–137: Nubble Light, York Beach, Maine

Page 139: Ferry, Inside Passage, Alaska

Pages 140–141: Wildwood, New Jersey

Pages 142–143: Long Beach, New Jersey

Page 144 (above): Sleeping Bear Dunes, National Lakeshore, Michigan

Page 144 (below): Boats, St. Simons Island, Georgia

Page 145: Sankaty Light, Nantucket Island, Massachusetts

Pages 146–147: Camden, Maine

Page 149 (above): Lobster fisherman, South Bristol, Maine

Page 149 (below): Crab fishermen, Crisfield, Maryland

Pages 150–151: Big Sur, California

Pages 152–153: Fort Jefferson National Monument, Dry Tortugas, Florida

Page 155: Hawaiian rowers, Hawaii

Pages 156–157: Pier, Hermosa Beach, California

Page 158: Camden, Maine

Page 159: Pebble Beach Golf Link, California

Page 160: Cape Sebastian, Oregon

Page 161: Portland Head Light, Maine

Pages 162–163: Rialto Beach, Olympic National Park, Washington

Afoot and lighthearted I take to the open road,

Healthy, free, the world before me,

The long brown path before me leading wherever I choose . . .

Strong and content, I travel the open road.

—Walt Whitman

ROADWAYS

Pages 164–165: Route 163, Monument Valley, Navajo Nation, Utah/Arizona

Pages 166–167: Route 163, Monument Valley, Navajo Nation, Utah/Arizona

Page 169: Kauai, Hawaii

Page 170: Stowe, Vermont

Page 171: Route 1, Big Sur, California

Page 172 (above): Gunnison, Colorado

Page 172 (below): Dusty road, Monument Valley, Navajo Nation, Utah

Page 173: Mt. St. Helens National Volcanic Monument, Washington

Page 175 (above): Route 240, Badlands National Park, South Dakota

Page 175 (below): Road, near Mexican Hat, Utah

Pages 176–177: Driving into the night, Nevada

Page 178: Eisenhower Expressway, Chicago, Illinois

Page 179: Kansas City, Missouri

Page 181 (above): Prescott, Arizona

Page 181 (below): Montgomery, Vermont

Page 182: Old Trace, Natchez Trace, Mississippi

Page 183: Mt. Tremper, New York

Page 184: White Mountains National Park, New Hampshire

Page 185: Highway 1, Big Sur, California

Pages 186–187: Sierra Nevada Mountains, California

Far below and around lay the city like a ragged purple dream,
the wonderful, cruel, enchanting, bewildering, fatal, great city.

—O. Henry

CITIES

Pages 188–189: Houston, Texas

Pages 190–191: Alamo Square, San Francisco, California

Page 193 (above): Palm Beach, Florida

Page 193 (below): Key West, Florida

Pages 194–195: Charleston, South Carolina

Page 196: Vietnam Veterans Memorial and Washington Monument, Washington, D.C.

Page 197: Lincoln Memorial and Washington Monument, Washington, D.C.

Page 199: Renaissance Center, Detroit, Michigan

Pages 200–201: Federal Reserve Building, Minneapolis, Minnesota

Page 202: Construction worker, Union, New Jersey

Page 203: Gateway Arch, St. Louis, Missouri

Page 204: Mission San Xavier del Bac, also called White Dove of the Desert, Tucson, Arizona

Page 205: Sculpture, Dallas, Texas

Page 207: French Quarter, New Orleans, Louisiana

Pages 208–209: The Confederate Monument, Forsyth Park, Savannah, Georgia

Page 210: Rock concert, Philadelphia, Pennsylvania

Page 211: New York Mets ticker tape parade, New York, New York

Pages 212–213: Albuquerque International Balloon Fiesta, New Mexico

No FT ... no comment

FT reac... new heig

Computer system

THE POST OFFICE is to introduce a computerised information network linking all of its main offices in an effort to speed up mail delivery.

Keever post

MR DEREK KEEVER has been appointed father of the year. Presenting Paula Keever, born on November 20 1987

US bank reorganises

London

The all-Chaikovsky concert presented under the auspices of the Royal Philharmonic Society at the Festival Hall on Wednesday night was a superior example of a much-abused genre

Chaikovsky/Festival Hall

The all-Chaikovsky concert presented under the auspices of the Royal Philharmonic Society at the Festival Hall on Wednesday night was a superior example of a much-abused genre Itzhak Perlman was the soloist in the Violin

Mr Naylor who joined the group in 1969, has been a dictator since 1986. He is also a non-executive director at Rest der Familie gruesst Stephanie Deharde in Germany. Ramtion of British Industry on the City Takeover Panel.

feed information on issues such as local traffic conditions and sorting office bottlenecks into central computer at Chesterfield in Derbyshire. The data will be used to help route delivery in the most effective way.

arm of US bank reorganises

FINANCIAL TIMES FT 1888 1988 CENTENARY YEAR

Page 215: New York City Marathon, Verrazano-Narrows Bridge, New York

Page 216 (above): Yankee Stadium, New York, New York

Page 216 (below): Finishing line, Kentucky Derby, Churchill Downs, Louisville, Kentucky

Page 217 (above): Lap 500, Indianapolis 500, Indiana

Page 217 (below): Notre Dame vs. Penn State, South Bend, Indiana

Page 218: Rodeo at Cheyenne Frontier Days, Wyoming

Page 219: Farmers market, Dallas, Texas

Pages 220–221: Cherry blossoms, Washington, D.C.

Page 223: Denver, Colorado

Page 224: First Interstate Bank Tower and Cumberland Hill School, Dallas, Texas

Page 225: John Hancock Tower with Trinity Church, Boston, Massachusetts

Page 226 (above): Pantheon, Nashville, Tennessee

Page 226 (below): Chicago, Illinois

Page 227: Miami Beach, Florida

Pages 228–229: United terminal, Chicago-O'Hare International Airport, Illinois

Page 231 (above): Three butchers, Newark, New Jersey

Page 231 (below): Band, Preservation Hall, New Orleans, Louisiana

Page 232 (above): Miss Teen USA Pageant, San Bernardino, California

Page 232 (below): Christmas lights, Queens, New York, New York

Page 233: Fremont Street, Las Vegas, Nevada

Page 234: Disneyland, Anaheim, California

Page 235: Statue of Liberty, New York, New York

Page 237: Empire State Building, New York, New York

Pages 238–239: Schuylkill River, Philadelphia, Pennsylvania

Pages 240–241: Dallas, Texas

Page 243: Washington, D.C.

Pages 244–245: Pittsburgh, Pennsylvania

Page 246 (above): State House, Providence, Rhode Island

Page 246 (below): State Capitol, Oklahoma City, Oklahoma

Page 247 (above): State Capitol, St. Paul, Minnesota

Page 247 (below): *Bronco Buster*, Denver, Colorado

Pages 248–249: Suburb, Houston, Texas

Page 251: Library of Congress, Washington, D.C.

Page 252: Empire State Building and Statue of Liberty, New York, New York

Page 253 (above): Eagle gargoyle, Chrysler building, New York, New York

Page 253 (below): World Trade Center Towers, New York, New York

Pages 254–255: "Future City"

ACKNOWLEDGMENTS

Thank you to all the Americans who have smiled and helped me. Pulled me out of sand and out of the ocean, put me in the air, sailed me on the water, and put me on their horses. The American has an open heart, and I'm grateful for that.

Special thanks to:

Alaska: Doug Geeting and Fritz and Anne Iversen

California: Alice Friedman and Sandy Segal

Delaware: Rico Allen, the Olsen family and Gigi Windley

Maryland: Lee Wilson

Montana: Ralph and Candice Miller

New York: Anne for her support, research and love, Bill Black, Bob Ciano, David Frist, Tony Gardner, Jim Good, Gilda Hannah, Nick Iversen, Eddie Millar, Grant Parrish, Joe Pobereskin, Chloe Rajs, Frances Rajs, Janina Rajs, Sam Rosalsky, Jordan Schapps, Jules Solo, Mark Speed, Pete Turner and Jimmy Winstead

Texas: Pete and Dorothy Grant, James Michener, Red McCoombs Ranch and the Y-O Ranch

Virginia: Greg Anderson

Wyoming: Bob and Elaine Walker
the people in the National Parks Service and the many state tourist and motion picture boards

Page 22: "Walking" by Henry David Thoreau, *Atlantic Monthly,* June 1862
Page 90: Speech on agriculture by Daniel Webster, The Boston State House, 1840
Page 134: "The Dry Salvages" (excerpt) by T.S. Eliot from *Four Quartets.* Copyright © 1943 by T.S. Eliot, copyright © 1935, 1936 by Esme Valerie Eliot. Reprinted by permission of Harcourt Brace Jovanovich Inc.
Page 164: "Song of the Open Road" (excerpt) by Walt Whitman, *Leaves of Grass,* 1855
Page 188: Strictly Business by O. Henry, 1910